My Flesh the Sound of Rain

Heather MacLeod
My Flesh the Sound of Rain

*for my dear friend
Michele in December 2017
here's looking at you
kid :)*

COTEAU BOOKS

All Poems © Heather MacLeod, 1998.

All rights reserved. No part of this book covered by the copyrights herein may be reproduced or used in any form or by any means – graphic, electronic or mechanical – without the prior written permission of the publisher. Any request for photocopying, recording, taping, or storage in information storage and retrieval systems of any part of this book shall be directed in writing to:
CanCopy, 6 Adelaide Street East, Suite 900, Toronto, Ontario, M5C 1H6.

Edited by Patrick Lane.
Cover and book design by Duncan Campbell.
Cover illustration by Bernice Friesen.
Author photo by Katy Ellis.
Printed and bound in Canada.

The excerpt from *What the Light Teaches* from *Miner's Pond*
by Anne Michaels and the excerpt from *Demon Pond* by Christopher
Dewdney, used by permission, McClelland & Stewart, Inc.
The Canadian Publishers.

The excerpt from *Afterworlds* by Gwendolyn MacEwan is used by permission
of the family of Gwendolyn MacEwan and McClelland & Stewart, Inc.
The Canadian Publishers.

The excerpt from *The Small Words in My Body* by Karen Connelly is used by
permission of Gutter Press.

The publisher gratefully acknowledges the financial assistance of the
Saskatchewan Arts Board, the Canada Council for the Arts,
the Department of Canadian Heritage, and the City of Regina
Arts Commission, for its publishing programme.

Coteau Books celebrates the 50th anniversary of
the Saskatchewan Arts Board with this publication.

Canadian Cataloguing in Publication Data

Macleod, Heather, 1964-
My flesh, the sound of rain
ISBN 1-55050-141-0

1. Title.
PS8575.L4625M9 1998   C811'.54   C98-920117-1
PR9199.3.M33425M9 1998

Coteau Books
401-2206 Dewdney Avenue
Regina, Saskatchewan
S4R 1H3

AVAILABLE IN THE U.S. FROM:

General Distribution Services
85 River Rock Road, Suite 202
Buffalo, New York,
USA, 14207

*For my mother, Mazie Ann Nelson
and my grandfather,
Simney Beeds,
who passed away in March of 1989.*

Contents

Part One: Places to Live

- 3 Words from my Mother
- 4 After a day in the Cariboo fields he falls asleep in the bath
- 6 My grandfather is dead
- 7 Shaman
- 8 The Youngest Child
- 10 The first time
- 12 Raspberries
- 14 Shilo
- 15 Moan Out Loud
- 17 To Marry an Angel
- 19 I look for a place to live
- 21 To look for something familiar
- 22 My mother is that
- 23 Touch the Buffalo
- 25 Through the Looking Glass
- 26 Another House
- 27 Original Sin
- 28 Cradle of my birth
- 29 Pomegranate
- 31 Reflection
- 32 The Bloody Chamber
- 34 Endurance
- 35 The Making of a Raven
- 36 Your name – Methusalah
- 38 Praise for the Crow
- 39 The Old Hag-Woman
- 40 I Have Lived Here Since The World Began
- 41 Fashioned

Part Two: Folded like a Map

- 45 Necropolis
- 47 I dream Rebecca a letter from Istanbul
- 48 Losing English
- 49 Efes
- 51 I think my mother a letter from Istanbul
- 52 Things I've learned with the turning of my hands
- 53 after having loved that country like blood burst in the brain
- 54 Escaping
- 56 The Sound of a Violin
- 57 After the Rain
- 59 In the Absence of God
- 62 The Wing of God named Noah
- 64 The world has too much colour
- 65 Smell Violets
- 66 God Made Fruit
- 68 On Marrying a Dragon
- 70 Marrying Snails
- 72 On Marrying the Last Unicorn
- 73 Apple Seeds
- 75 Up Against the Wall, Mother
- 76 Birthmarks
- 78 you bring out the good girl in me
- 79 In the Presence of Your Heart
- 81 I swear it to you
- 83 Cover Me with Kisses

Part Three: Too Small to Remember

- 87 What I want
- 88 My mother taught me
- 90 I want to go home
- 91 I loved her
- 92 Compass
- 93 When I'm dead

The name of the night our mouths nibbling
the dark bread of love the dark flowers of love

– Gwendolyn MacEwan

Part 1: Places to Live

When there are no places left for us,
we'll still talk in order to make things true:
not only the years before we were born,
not only the names of our dead,
but also this life.
The simple feel of an apple in the hand.

– Anne Michaels

Words from my Mother

A lack of pleasure makes you clumsy;
dreaming of watermelons is a sign of pregnancy,
                        are you pregnant?
Don't open tin cans upside down
it's bad luck, and never buy a rocking chair
only the dead'll sit in it;
when that old Labrador howls at the full moon
I'll be dead; see those three black crows,
the ones on the left side of the road?
They're good luck, but six on the right are bad.
If a bird flies into your house someone's sick,
and if it lands before it flies out then someone is dying.
      You never touched Grandpa after he was dead,
do you think he doesn't know?
If you want to get rid of your company
put your broom behind the back door,
and make sure it's upside down.
      They say, the old women can fly
from the fat of an unbaptized child,
but you're not pregnant
                        are you?

After a day in the Cariboo fields he falls asleep in the bath

The smell of hay and horses living inside his nose,
never going away, simply there, like the scar beside his right ear,
the one he got when he came home drunk, stumbled
and fell on his chainsaw. He was embarrassed in the morning,
the smell of beer and cigarettes fresh on his breath.
Stitches raised and gleaming with blood like glowing
red beads in the shapes of flowers on her moccasins.

In the evening he comes out to the kitchen,
bare feet against the cold black and white checkered linoleum,
steam like ice fog rolling towards us, winding its way
along his edges, *I fell asleep in the bath,* he tells her.
His hands prune-like from the water,
and she has her white, green striped coffee mug in her hand,
half-way to her mouth when she asks, *What did you dream?*

Last Christmas I was in Istanbul, spent the morning
curled up in a bath not much bigger than an old washing tub.
I thought about my grandmother, the one who raised
me till I was ten and never asked what I dreamt,
even when I lied one morning
and told her I'd fallen asleep in the bath.
But at night under the chill of fresh flannel sheets
I dreamt of babies (small like mewling kittens)
bobbing in oceans, round and global, silent as death.

There's nothing like coming in from the cold
of a winter night in the Cariboo,
with the men left to clean the rabbits, moose or deer
from hunting or trapping, and I'd wash my hands
in the hot water of my grandmother's kitchen sink;
I'd push my hands and arms into the water up to my elbows,
and the women would be busy cooking or baking,
and I'd take one of my grandma's old, checkered tea towels,
and press it against my face and smell my family
from the width of their hips to the freckles
caressing their cheeks and backs.
I remember the very best of them and of her, my grandmother,
who told me and my girl cousins, as she peeled yellow apples,
I used to dream of trees, tall in the fields taking up space
from the sky, and instead of green leaves
the willows, oaks, and pines had green babies.

My grandfather is dead

My grandfather is dead –
I swallow his eyes
to see what he saw.

I take his hands and sew them
into my breasts so he will always hold me,
know my body as it swells for a child.
I want him there to feed my children,
know their mouths, their hunger.

Shaman

I spread wild flowers and feathers
over your grave,
dance wildly, my arms spread out
and sometimes I scream.
I only make it rain.

I bend my body pretending to be old,
hold sticks in my arms
and toss them by the river's edge.
Come on old man, I whisper,
get up from your bed.

I paint my face with charcoal,
do cartwheels and sing.
I kill muskrats and rabbits,
think the smell of blood
will tickle your nose.

Old man, rise from your grave
kick the earth from your feet.
Old man, there's still
life in your bones.

But even as I speak
you flutter to dust,
settle on my boots.

So
I step carefully.

The Youngest Child

The things my brother taught me came in soft spots
like the top of a baby's head,
a place you love to move your fingers
tingling the soft peach fuzz of the newly born.
He filled my mind with words you could tell
he thought were magic, pulled them out of his mouth
like the sacred, like the holy strum,
the thick throated pluck of a cello.

I offered him pale flowers.
After our sister's death, I gave him the words
cyclamen and azaleas.
Saw the flowers ivory shapes in the pupil
of each eye. Imagined the shape,
the sound of *cyclamen and azaleas*.
The words made room behind his eyes
between plate tectonics and silicate minerals.

He followed me out of the Kootenays,
and threw his worn, canvas backpack
in the trunk. Underneath his arm
he carried an old, bent, library-stolen
copy of Jack Keroauc's *On The Road*.
I had turned eighteen that summer,
left with the scent of my sister's
cyclamen and azaleas still on my fingers,
and with my high school boyfriend
who carried an equally worn, bent
copy of Rilke's *Letters To A Young Poet*.

I felt as if I had, by choice, allowed
my body to change and separate me
from my brother by so much more than age.

I missed my sister, and thought
as we drove back and forth down Denver's
main road looking for relics of a past
which pre-dated all our births,
I suffered this alone.
Somewhere between the Grand Canyon
and California with the word *solace*
moving around *cyclamen and azaleas*,
I threw my brother's stolen, bent book
out the window and refused to be sorry.
Refused to give in regardless of the taps
to the back of the seat which worked into kicks
and which, in turn, inspired my vocal chords
to rise three octaves above anything considered
normal, resulting in their palpable silence,
until I wondered if only dogs could hear me.

With the car sitting empty at the side of the road,
with my brother and boyfriend searching
for the library-stolen, worn copy of Keroauc's
On The Road I paced the shoulder and walked the line.
I spotted the book in the ditch and crawled
in and out of the dirt to rescue my brother's
solace, something I had realized
far too late, and was at last silent.

I spent the rest of the day in the back seat.
In the late afternoon my brother turned to me
holding a paper bag of fruit toward me,
and I asked him if the bag was filled with oranges.
He said, his mouth full, *Satsumas and Mandarins*.
I reached in and when I looked at him
he smiled and said, *Cyclamen and azaleas*.

The first time

I was young
       with my sister lying quietly
amid too many apologies for a young girl
and I carried the guilt for my
                      well being
in my hands and my hair
       which I cut close to my scalp;
I wanted to number her somehow
                      among the many.

The first time I spent all night with him
I waited until he was asleep,
and then I held my wrists before me
       blue roads
                      clear, unmarked
       and well traveled.

I sat beside her through her second spinal tap;
       I think much worse than the first
                      made familiar,
       and expected.
I read her poetry our Grandfather had written,
and thought how the loveliest parts of the human body
                      were the wrists.
       So pale and delicate

she came home from the hospital
asked us to call her Skinhead,
       so sure it would be her nickname in school.
And she wanted to know everything,
       and what I didn't know I made up;
elaborate tales fit for the Brothers Grimm
and late in the evenings my mind filled

with fiction and mythical geography
I met him in the high school field
       still I remember the smell
       of his high school jacket
       and the low, calm touch of leather.

The first time he brought me flowers
I took them to her and she rolled her eyes
tired, she said, *of the smell of the grave.*
I held her hands and told her how late
in the evenings I lied in the fields staring at the night
as it fell toward me and held me against
fresh cut grass, and these flowers
were given with passion, with the desire
and the need for flesh.

In Grade Three I found out my veins carried blood,
and I ran home to tell her. I traced the veins
along her hands, and she held her wrists out to me,
This is my blood, she said, and I kissed first one wrist
                           and then the other.
After she died I crawled into bed with her;
I covered our bodies with the sheets of the hospital,
and I ran my fingertips over her wrists,

            and through his hair;
I told him the blood in my family was strong;
then I curled up in the grass
                     the soft blades against my face
and I held my wrists out and I said:
                This is my blood.

Raspberries
for my brother, Kevin

I

We're born without maps
how can we figure out where we are?
She apologized, once, for giving birth to us,
and sat on the kitchen chair, in her left hand
a scrub brush, crying.
I said nothing, neither did my brother,
what else could we do, we washed the floor.

Later we went hunting for raspberries,
and found small, blood red buds.
They were juicy to eat but tart on the tongue,
and when she ate them, she forgot about
the badness of the world, she forgot,
but we remembered
the sweet, tart goodness of raspberries.

II

As children we spent our summers
at Meadow Lake. Absorbed, by the water,
we learned to live at the lakeside,
close to plants, animals, each other.
My brother found a bird in the field.
She'd pretend her wing was broke
to lure him away from her nest.
He wasn't fooled and found her eggs.
I leaned over as he held one of the small,
cream-coloured, spotted eggs in his right hand.
He broke it gingerly, spilling what was inside,
so we could look at it. I didn't like it.

In the tent he brought raspberries
to take away the bitter taste.
We fell asleep beside one another,
a bucket of raspberries in the middle.
I woke because I could feel something
moving in my hair, it crawled across my head,
down my arm, moved through my fingers
onto my brother's stomach.
It was a small green lizard, it curled up in the hollow
of his belly button and I watched them sleep.

III

We travel without maps, my brother and I,
we move around the country without direction,
to follow the feel of the road.
We ignore the signs that will only lead
us in the wrong direction.
He lives in the north on the south side
of Great Slave Lake
              somewhere he's eating raspberries,
lying in the hot sun, tiny, green lizards
moving in and out of the centre of his flesh.

Shilo

My sister, Claire, comes to visit me in the summer. I'm living in the Yukon, and Claire flirts with my boyfriend Chris. She asks if I'll come home next spring. I'm not sure what spring has to do with it, and I don't answer her. I find a dog and we name her Shilo after a Neil Diamond song our mom used to sing.

I live in a small cottage everyone calls a shack, out by Takhini Hot Springs. It doesn't have electricity or plumbing. Claire hates the honey bucket. I spend most of my time with the dog.

I decide to leave Chris. Although, *leave Chris* is a funny term, after all, it's not like I ever arrived at Chris, but anyway I decide to leave him. After I've left Chris and I decide to meet for the token-friendship-lunch-of-exlovers and Claire insists on coming.

Over lunch I'm being cryptic and searching for the right amount of pain with the slight nuance of tragedy and resilience. I think I've about mastered it when I notice my socks don't match. I take this to be a sign of legitimate pain, tragedy and a lack of resilience; I begin talking about my dog. Claire staggers my imagination with her rambling on Café au Lait versus Latté. I didn't know there was a difference. Chris is mesmerized by Claire's rambling. I notice their feet entwined under the table. Their socks match.

Chris and Claire spend the summer together, and before Claire leaves on the plane to go home she thanks me. I try to remember anything and everything our mother ever said to us about family and love, and I'm about to settle for one of our mother's Irish phrases littered with obscenities, instead I pet my dog and I say to my sister, *It was my pleasure.*

Moan Out Loud

My sister, Claire, tells the story
while we're driving from Prince George to Vancouver.
She says they were bored one night,
and so they began to trim one another's hair.
Pacatchi hair. She tells me
how he trimmed each strand,
and when he was done cutting
he pulled on her hair with his teeth.
He kissed her, touched her with his tongue
until she pulled at his head,
until she moaned out loud.

She asks if I've ever moaned out loud.
I roll my eyes like our mother,
Of course. Moan out loud
all the time I think, moan out loud,
before I have to go to the dentist, moan out loud,
every time I try to balance my cheque book,
before and after every ride on the Ferris Wheel,
moan out loud, every time we go visit our grandmother,
every time our sister, Hannah, comes to visit me,
and once a month when I get cramps, I let a small
                moan out loud.
Christ,
moan out loud?

When? she asks me.

I shrug, tell her I couldn't begin to count
all the times I've moaned out loud.
That many? she asks, and like a fool I nod my head,
and so she says, *Tell me one.*

What to do?
Should I tell her about the time
I backed into a police car?
Possibly the largest and longest moan.
What about the time as a teenager
when I drank vodka straight?
You can't think of one? she rolls her eyes,
challenges me until I'm sure I have no choice,
so I tell her about living in the cottage
on Denman Island. She's bored, heard it all before.
I tell her, *He came home from the drugstore,
and I don't remember what he said,
but I went to him and we were rough with each other.
We actually broke the kitchen door.
I've never felt anything like it before.
I felt like I lost a part of myself,
with or without him I would always be less
having known him.
I was anonymous and unformed until he came into me.*

Wow, she's impressed,

and it's too late because I see him,
he throws open the door, raging.
No comfort, no compassion, instead it's
an accusation that hangs in the air.
I want to kill him, want to squash
the life out of him. We break the kitchen door,
and he makes me cry out loud.

How come you left him? she asks,
and so I tell her the truth. At the end,
he made me moan out loud.

To Marry an Angel

She's young, six or seven,
and my brother calls her flaxen-haired.
I'm not sure if I like her; I don't know her,
but her eyes remind me of ancestors
in the old photographs hanging
in my grandmother's parlour.
There is something about her like the old
women in the country,
the ones who pour honey and milk
in the fields hoping the crops will grow.

She asks what I'll be when I grow up,
and for a moment and several more
I cannot imagine. *What will I be?*
I'll be a Buddhist, I tell her
though I'm not sure how to, even, spell it.
She nods, though it's clear she's only slightly
satisfied, *What'll you marry?* she asks.
I'm supposed to marry a Turkish man, I tell her,
though I've avoided his calls for weeks.
She purses her lips and tries to whistle then tells me,
You will not marry Turkey.
I nod my head and I, too, purse my lips
and attempt to whistle. This, at least,
is one thing we have in common.
You, she tells me as she points her index finger,
slick with grease from her french fries,
will marry an angel.

I think of all those Sunday sermons
angels carrying war, famine, disease
and death curled in one hand,
and, always, one pristine, pale wing dipped
in the blood of God's desire.

I think I will marry Turkey, I tell her,
thinking how rude it is to avoid calls.
That's too late, she says, rolling her eyes;
her old woman's hand inching towards my rootbeer
which I pick up before she has a chance.
Maybe I'll be the one to marry an angel, she looks hopeful,
as if she can see Raphael's fat cherubs descending.
She isn't afraid of a being who will go from lamb to lion,
who has instigated conception with a whisper to the ear,
and will crack a gold seal to release
a sun black as sackcloth
and a moon red as blood. She's my brother's child,
so I tell her, *Stay away from angels,
remember, Lucifer's an angel too.*

I look for a place to live

I wear newsprint
on my fingertips,
and cut mangos
into tiny square chunks
of moist flesh.
I decide not to buy anything else,
even toilet paper.
Instead I steal it
from friends and restaurants.

When I see a blank piece of paper
I write my name
over and over.

Sometimes I reorganize
the letters,
so it isn't my name
except to me.

I would give him everything,
but he never asks.

When he tells me,
quiet, he doesn't love me
I rush about wildly,
shutting all the doors,
but I leave the windows open.
I let the breeze ripple across my body,
new things to feel.

Claire comes over,
and I stuff her
in a corset from
the 15th century.
Her breasts press
against whalebone.
I take photographs of her,
and mix them with
photographs of headstones
from west coast graveyards.
We pack up my things
and I go home with her to mother's.
It is Beltane.
Claire and I begin a bonfire
to welcome back the Virgin.
I paint the wounds
of Christ on her body.
It looks real, she tells me.
Our mother comes in
and tells us it is Beltane
not Easter.

How do you feel people, I ask.
How do you miss people, I ask
I'm not sure, I tell them.
No, I'm not sure.

To look for something familiar

I paint the outline of my body on the floor and lie inside the chalked shape of who I am. I paint my sister's nude body for Samhain turning her small breasts into eyes, our mother laughs and bites her nails; I dress up as Wednesday Addams and get sick of the snapping of my own fingers.

After the women died in Montréal my mother still wanted to eat her birthday cake, but I said we couldn't. Instead we went outside and on the street I painted the white outline of my sister's body in various poses fourteen times.

When my family leaves in the morning I get up and paint as many things as I can; my sister comes home early and I paint her nude body and then photograph her juxtaposed against the various scenes in the house. I like it when they come home, but don't recognize anything except me. I want them to feel like I feel. I want everything to be suspect.

My mother is that

My mother is that
blue mountain
Grandfather built from scratch using
his tendons and ligaments,
he stretched and pulled and planted
his seeds.

My mother is that
never to-be-ripe pumpkin
Grandmother made using
the peelings of her yellowed flesh
and scraps of her skin.

My mother is that
clump of dulled amber
her lovers made using
their dried sperm
and the tip of their wet hunger.

My mother is that
swan God made using
angels wings he pulled
from their spines,
the smooth crack
and the red, red blood.

Touch the Buffalo

When I left,
my brother came with me,
the only way he knew
to make sure I'd keep coming home.

Leaving,
we made the words we wouldn't
hear in the southern part of our country.
We poured them off our tongues:
Inuit, Inuvialuit, Tuktoyaktuk,
Dene, Dogrib, inukshuk, ulu,
mukluk, Inuktitut, Pangnirtung, Iqaluit.
They dripped off and into the dry
dust of the road from Yellowknife
to Fort Providence.

We saw herds of bison,
we saw muskox and black bears
and Elizabeth drinking beer
in Hay River, her Bronco bent.

The bison followed us out
of the Northwest Territories.
They wanted me to touch them.
At the border, with my brother
asleep in the truck, I did.

I touched the bison,
wanted them to remember me.

When I come home
I greet the bison at the border,
in my mind I say my brother's name,
I say, *Buffalo*
and realize I've been gone too long.

My home has been divided
between the Dene and Inuit.
My brother and Elizabeth dance slowly
in the Strange Range their bodies close,
multiplying the distance.

The words and the languages of my home
seem strange on my tongue.
The syllabics of Inuktitut look only
like odd symmetrical shapes

An elder tells me I should chew
on the dirt. I should run my tongue
over my land.

Through the Looking Glass

Try these on, my sister says to me

and she lights another cigarette even though she doesn't like smoking. He used to and now she smokes for him. She wears his old clothes, jackets, flannel shirts, wool socks, even his boxer shorts sometimes.

Claire, I say, *I want to throw it all away. All of these things which marked who he was and where he came from and who he'd loved or had known.* She just smiles at me, shaking her head and pulls up his thick wool socks, they go all the way to her knees. I persist, *Everything. None of it is mine, none of it belongs to me. How do we hang onto something which doesn't belong to us, shouldn't be ours?* I am going to throw it all away except

she passes me his glasses, thick, black frames. There's nothing wrong with my eyesight, but I wear them anyway;

now nothing looks as good as it used to.

Another House

She built the house for my brother,
and left me and my sisters in the forest
to go wild. *Untameable,* she said.
Threw her dead babies out to us for food,
and made us bring her wood for the fire.

I crept close to the house,
leaned against her walls,
my back pressed against
the red brick.
I watched the flickering blackness
through her windows.
My brother pressed
his smooth, unmarked face
against the glass
and stretched his hand out,
his fingers pushing against
her house.

She threw him out one day,
and told me to take care of him.
He was weak and flabby,
his hair long and shining black.
Everywhere he put his foot
the earth would creak and bleed.

Later she wanted him back,
but by then I couldn't find him.
Instead I gave her some bones,
and she built a little puppet.
Close enough, she said.

Original Sin

I say, *I'll clean it*,
and I strip the incestuous bed,
pile linen in the hall,
gather dirty laundry,
throw it on top of the linen.
I pull open closet doors,
gather old clothes for the Salvation Army.
I take paintings and prints from the walls,
gather photographs of my father and mementos,
tie them together in a plastic bag.
Friends and acquaintances come by,
they pick through prints and paintings,
they finger my belongings,
Can I have, they ask me,
and take away plants,
books, a soft coloured vase with hearts on it.
They gather magazines, old purses
and sweat shirts, and leave, bundled down, smiling.
I do the laundry, fold the linen and clothes.
My mother comes by for the bedding,
and my brother brings me an apple,
we cut it so the pentacle shines
and we eat.
He checks my tires and my mother weeps.
I have begun my journey.
I have begun.

Cradle of my birth

My brother has found
the cradle of his birth,
our grandfather fashioned it
from old twisted apple trees,
it was hard to shape
like us all.

Not long after my birth
my body enticed my father
like a will of its own.
It bent, warped and wrapped
its way through his imagination.
It must have known how it made him feel
with his teeth and his tongue,
and his mouth
so hungry.

My father made it
and I am too old
to be displeased.
I am too old
to point the finger,
to wag the tongue
to bury
the secrets.

This then is the cradle
of my birth.

Pomegranate

I peel back the years to you, Father,
layers of my skin,
or layers from pieces of fruit,
thick skin from oranges,
uncover the sweetness
of five-year-old flesh.

I peel back the years to 1969,
when mother wore
long, flowered dresses
and loved Jefferson Airplane,

but you, Father, twisted me
like the stem of an apple;
you divided me like a pomegranate,
chewed on my insides;
Father you bit into me
and forced me to take you
into the mouth I owned in 1969.

I peel back the years to you, Father.
And I have not been five for over 20 years,
but I feel her in my mouth
the child-heart shaped like a strawberry.
She likes to spit,
can never be rid of your seed,
Father. I can never get rid of you.

I crack myself like melons
against sidewalks, don't step
on the crack, and I run myself,
cherry juice over men,
whose passions push you
around in my mind like the hard,
silver disc in a pinball machine.
I thought all men took women
unwilling, wanted them that way.
I thought all men loved like you,
Father, loved with rape in one hand,
and a pomegranate in the other.
Something sweet to promise me
before they split me, peeled me back.

Reflection

She comes from all the blood,
made from all the secrets,
she buries the truth, tries to hide it from me.
Does she remember
what she's done with it?
Where did she put the things
which really happened?

Late at night I steal the truth from her.
It's precious I tuck it into the corners
of the room, and under the covers.
And late at night, I tape my legs together
winding the tape from hip to ankle,
but she parts them when I'm not looking.

I get up from her body, and I gather the truth
from the corners.
I pull out my birth certificate,
trace my name and my birth-date.
Smell the paper,
lick the name of the city
I was born in.
I cut my father out –
cut my father's name out,
large hole in this paper,
large hole.

The Bloody Chamber

Before I was born
I lived in his testicles.
I was the first.
I swam stroke after stroke to reach the egg.
I grew up with a good sense of humour
and no sense for direction.

After me came Hannah, Claire,
and the twins Kevin and Kile.

Two years after our father had left the house,
Hannah invited him for dinner.
She said we'd get better if we'd just
sit down together and eat,
but she couldn't cook him dinner.
When he came to the house there wasn't any food.
We sat in the living room pretending
we hadn't watched our mother leave,
driving erratically, waving her arms at the neighbours.
Father sat in her favourite chair nodding his head.

I poured him red wine
and put on his favourite tape,
but I couldn't talk to him.
Claire sat cross-legged on the floor
reading *The Bloody Chamber*
she didn't speak, didn't look at us.
Hannah stayed in the kitchen
almost, so it seemed, about to cook.
Kevin and Kile sat across from father,
they looked out the window, to the kitchen,
over to Claire and finally at me.

When our father left, Kevin got drunk
and sat in the truck with Grandpa's 22.
I stood at the window
with my sisters and we watched
Kile tap on the window,
and the two people my father
never raped comforted one another.

Before I was born
I lived in his testicles,
crowded with the damp and moist;
I pushed my way out.
I was the first.
I held my hands in front of me
my teeth clenched,
      semen everywhere.

Endurance

    I am angry with her   again;
it's because my father sits between us,
his mouth dripping blood like an hyena,
and his breath poisoning the air.

    And some days I greet her with fire;
a rage so intense it startles me from the rafters,
until I'm pulled into my body, the uncomfortable
snap of an elastic band against my mind.

    I want to say I'm over being raped
by her husband; I want to say I'm a survivor
but I can't help rolling my eyes at the mere thought;
I want to say I forgive her for not knowing but I can't.

    Truly, most days I seldom think of it, and I give
God the blame for how I have been made instead of
placing it in the past, and I cross the words victim
and survivor from my vocabulary and I live the word
endurance, like a dog with a bone who refuses to give up.

The Making of a Raven

       I am so cold I can't remember why I came
so far to be here; can't imagine what I could have
been thinking. I put ads in the local newspapers,
but nobody answers me. I tell them I am lost
and sleeping, the only material possessions
I have from the past are these two worn, thin
tapes of Simon and Garfunkel. I must have liked them.

       I am so cold I remember the smells and sounds
of horses, how my fingers would tangle in their manes
and my feet would dangle loosely from the stirrups.
I remember how I would ride Appaloosas from the rising
of the stars into the falling of the sun. My hair still
smells of hay and nightfall.

       I am so cold I pull myself inwards until
like the child I was long ago my cheeks freckle,
my bones move the other direction into scuffed knees
and the automatic jump of skipping rope.

       I am so cold I follow the ravens to the graveyard,
and paint myself with henna and charcoal as the rough
kwa kwa of the raven tells me, and I fall asleep
in a shallow grave, the permafrost closing my mind.

Now my wings beat back the cold and my eyes
wink out the past in a beat of a lash and if I could
      I'd smile.

Your name – Methusalah

I thought if I saw you again I'd say:

Listen, years ago I called your name,
sang it over the Tundra from Taloyoak
as you left, with the other Inuit,
to go on the land. You left the town
silent and dead, except for Whitemen
who roamed like nomads.
I called your name long after your shape
was indistinct on the horizon.
I was sure I could still see you,
the shape of you the same as my fist,
and I was afraid. Frightened of Inuit legends
about nomads who come across the ice,
look like friend but take pieces of you –
slowly like White hunters who roam
across other lands with rifles
and laughter on their lips. I was afraid,
for you left me in Taloyoak with all the White people,
told me I'd be all right and said, *You're Half-White*.
You ignored the shaking of my head and hands,
put your fist over my mouth and I wondered
which part of me you hated most, the Cree or the White.

But then I saw you again and said:

Remember when you left me in Taloyoak,
how the town emptied of Inuit? How you all
spotted the tundra like moving inukshuks,
shapes for your own people? I imagined you
on the land, without me, eating seal and whale meat raw.
The land pulled you as if the tundra itself moved your feet,
emptied you of everything. I tried to wait but I, too,
could feel my own people calling me south.
I could smell my grandfather's worn snowshoes,
his cold bannock and dried fish; I needed him
to fill me up with his Indian blood, but I left too late.
And your words came after me, have followed
me through the years. I am only Half.
Maybe the nomads took pieces of me; maybe
they could tell I wasn't whole; maybe as you hung
your head over the blood of a whale they hung
their heads over me and said, *She is only Half-White*,
and then began to eat.

Praise for the Crow
> *After Carla Funk's poem "Praise for the Zebra"*

Because you shimmer midnight blue in the sun,
hide layers of indigo and violet beneath the moon,
and have tapped me on the shoulder with your wing.

Because when my grandfather was dying,
his breath breaking from his chest
in small, shallow bursts,
you flew level with the open window of my car,
and said to me, *Call them*.

Because you have no shame and no regret.

Because my mother says six of you
on the right side of the road are bad luck,
and I like to see you lined up and shining
looking down at all the people moving
beneath you, driving and walking into
the charcoal folds of your luck.

Because my cousin, Kaug, caught you
when we were in the fifth grade.
He took you out of his make-shift cage,
with all the gentleness he had in his ten-year-old hands,
and with Grandpa's razor he sliced your tongue
knowing you'd be able to talk.
                    And you did.

Because you're tattooed on the inside of my ankle.

Because I let you loose from Kaug's make-shift cage;
I sent you flying, laughing and talking into the air.

The Old Hag-Woman

Old Hag-Woman built her home in trees,
lived by the easiest means possible.
Old Hag just wants to be free.
She says: *Take another lover,*
only another can know you.

I skip pebbles on the lake
and make sounds like the crows,
the beaks sharp, long and impossibly black.
No one knows I'm Indian unless I tell them,
but they call my brother Chief.
He grows his black hair long
and I touch the curls
that fall down his back.
In the summer he wears charcoal
under his eyes and down his nose;
he tells me he will scare away the sun.
It won't matter if I darken my skin,
I am still blonde and my eyes
will always be green. My brother laughs at me
and tells me I'm White.

I climb the trees in the Shuswap forest
until Old Hag-Woman finds me.
Her back is bent and her hair
whiter than my skin. She laughs,
talks about my father,
tells me things no one knows but me.
I say it was the whiskey that made him
the way he was. She shakes her head.
When I leave her I decide to live simply,
and I refuse for the longest time
to take anyone into my bed.

I Have Lived Here Since The World Began

She walks behind me
and says, *No one has stepped here.*
I turn back
see her standing in the hollows
of where I had, just moments before,
placed my own feet.
She says, *No one has stepped on this ground
until now.* She says,
I have walked on land no one else has.
She stands wobbling in the marsh of the tundra,
still in the hollows of where I had my own feet.
I turn away. I want to see what she sees.
The tundra's vastness makes it shrink
in on itself, and her European blood
makes her blind. As if she knows what I think
she says, *A piece of me is Algonquin,* she tilts her head,
What piece of you is Cree?
I kneel down in the marsh texture, my knees trembling,
and put my hands over my feet.
Not my feet. What's under them,
I tell her, *That part. The part that pushes me forward.*
The part that carries me across land,
the part that drums into my veins and makes my heart beat.
Then I tell her, *We have walked this land before.*
We are the crow who sang this land into its beginnings,
and the one who spit the sand out and made
these islands in this ocean called the tundra.

We've been here since the world began.

Fashioned

I am made like a crucifixion
complete with – violent beauty,
the bowed back of objection,
translucent eyes of suffering and grief
with the pull of flesh against metal.

I am made like a drug intervention
complete with – too much coffee and
steadfast strangers scattered on furniture,
unwavering acquaintances dispersed
between awkward silences, and the resolute
friends and family close-fisted together
their gossip palpable.

I am made like a drive-by-shooting
complete with – the breakneck spin
of the steering wheel,
the rapid run of the tires,
the ambulance, paramedics,
witnesses that saw nothing,
lamenting family and despairing friends.
I'm made like the clamorous crowd
illuminated in their pale misery,
with my hands held up, cast wide open
each finger an exclamation.

I am made like the crow and raven
complete with – murder and unkindness;
the fold of blue sky on sapphire, indigo over cobalt;
the foreign surrender of wing against wind.
I live in melody, in the moments unaware
of everything but the tang of redemption.

I am made like a sparrow
complete in the resonance of my hymn,
the motion of my body,
the way one moment bleeds into the next.
I was made in the presence of God
like liquid light pulled from the ether
I was formed in exquisite virtue,
with wisdom scarcely touching a wing.

Part2: Folded like a Map

*My hands and mouth travel
weightless and eager
over your radiant flesh.*

  – Christopher Dewdney

Necropolis

I know things in pieces.
I tell lies. Too much of me
can be found in the truth.
The things that are important
I hide between the lines
and wear shrouded around me,
the layers of what it means to become old.
What it means to lose and to regret
is the holy spark of compassion
in the black pupil of the eye.

When I was pregnant
I named the foetus Suzanne,
and listened to Bob Marley
and the light husk of another heart beat.
She would inherit everything from me
because I had made her by myself,
pinned as I was under the enraged power,
limited by the frailty of his sex.
She would like sunflowers and rain,
she would listen to Leonard Cohen, Bach, me.

I curled up in my mother's bed,
in the chamber of the woman
who conceived me, and my cousin came in,
sat beside me and talked about Kirk and Bones.
His forehead so carefully creased
with his own gentle worry.
When I went to the bathroom my body
rained, released blood notes wavering
in thin toilet water,
the sounds of sunflowers.
I was empty, and no matter what I did
I couldn't get full.

My cousin came in,
looked at what was left of me,
It's no good, he said
and I told him, *I am an orphan.*

I dream Rebecca a letter from Istanbul

Rebecca, when I come to lie in your arms
I'll be pregnant with Türkiye.
The one I give birth to I'll present to you,
let you cradle the mysteries of Islam,
let you hold the division and the joining
of Asia and Europe in your heart.

I will shrink away from Canada
leaving you the namesake of my country.
I'll give you and Canada
the best I can give, the slow, sweeping,
hazel eyes of a Muslim child.

When I come to lie in your arms,
I'll bring the Bosphorus Strait
running through my veins;
the Golden Horn between my breasts;
the shape and sounds of all I cannot know
of this country in my breath.
Carry its soil underneath my fingernails;
its blood, bone, and flesh in my womb.

When I come to lie in your arms,
I'll need a sister to brush
the tangles from my hair,
smooth the lines from my forehead,
still the wringing of my hands.

Run a hot bath for me, Becca.
I'm mad for Türkiye;
in love with Istanbul.
It pins me under the weight
of the five Islamic prayers,
has made me less than Canadian,
less than Turkish.

Losing English

Today I say I love you
in Turkish, *Seni seviyorum*.
I don't know if I mean it.
Would it be different
if I said it in English?

I lose my own language
as if it's written on a slip of paper
I continuously misplace.
The English I speak is broken
as if I, like you, spoke it second.

At night as I watch you sleep
I whisper, *Seni sevmekten korkuyorum*
       I'm afraid to love you.
I imagine myself ironing you out,
starching you like a white, cotton shirt
which smells of Tide and Downy,
and has been dried in the Canadian sun.

I imagine slipping you over
my freckled shoulders,
buttoning you over my appendix scar;
making you Canadian through association.
Today I whisper, *Seni seviyorum,*
and when you kiss me
I feel English slip out.

Efes

In Efes you walked ahead of me
running and posing for the camera,
and I saw you with one eye open,
and twisted you in and out of focus.
You were clear to me only for a flash.

I didn't want to leave Turkey,
and I wanted something in the middle.
A place where I could put one foot
on the cusp of Asia and Europe
and the other in Canada's rich soil.

In Efes my feet wore patterns in the dust,
the earth carried too much past,
and while I leaned against an ancient column
I found a snail shell.
A strange gift from Efes, curled up, small
and twisted on my palm.
I wanted to clutch too much.

Instead I opened my hands,
spread my fingers like wings,
let that country slip through
my opened hands like water.

When I left Turkey I packed all I had
and placed the beautiful in my backpack,
afraid to lose those things I'd be able to touch.
The sweater hand-knit by a Bedouin woman
rolled up in the bottom; neither it nor I
able to feel Turkey all the way in Canada.

I should have laid myself in the palm
of your hand curled like a shell,
and never asked how to get home.
Instead I watched you with one eye open
and felt movement between us,
> in and out of focus.

I think my mother a letter from Istanbul

Lay out pale seeds from oranges
and when they're dry from the sun
bury them with me.
Lay coins from Türkiye
over my eyes,
cut my heart
from my chest
bury it at the foot of an oak tree.
In death I will not bend.
Roots carve out valleys
in my cold heart.
And mother,
take the flesh from these hands;
hands that touched
and loved him so well;
burn my flesh on a pillar
sprinkled with lavender
and tender words I can never hear.
Take me from Türkiye, Mother,
bring me back to Canada.
You'll recognize my face,
I will be too still.
Tell him no one will love him
as well as me,
but leave him nothing.
Take even my memory,
feel it like a bird
moving in the palm
of your hand.
I've been gone so long;

I never thought I could return.

Things I've learned with the turning of my hands

> – just as my grandmother turned dough for bread
> the flour slick on her fingers, white blood –

I spread my legs like you ask. Your voice a sore,
a pale, red sliver which slides along the white powder of my skin.
I could name myself after common food
Grandma made from early morning to late afternoon.
I want you to name me; name the soft flesh
on the inside of my thighs; good, solid thighs,
thighs which have pressed against
the freckled coat of an Appaloosa;
wide hips; the rough, prickly red of my pubic hair,
copper pennies against fine, granulated sugar.

I spread my legs, feel the indent of your thumbs,
your index fingers against cinnamon buns,
banana loaf, angel-food cake, and baking powder biscuits,
the insistent press of you. I turn you over with my hands.
I feel you; I am curious, spread my legs to allow you.
Turn you over; touch you with what I am,
and carry with me the fine, granulated textures
from my grandmother; the smell of tea and Irish Loaf
                                        on her cool breath.

after having loved that country like blood burst in the brain

I left it in a dive like a hawk as it goes for a dove
smooth arc of air against pupils
dilating   cool in the spring heat   soft rush of desire
to be nowhere and everywhere at one single moment
and I was

with you in Turkey and left floating
in space above oceans and countries and   nothing
landed small and forgotten in Canada
the soft malt touch of rain against my eyes
closed against too much that was strange
too much familiar   too much forgotten

remembered I almost married you
wanted to in that other place that loved me
so well   cradled me   a lost child
warm milk against my mouth soft flesh against my fingers
wanted to give Turkey something back
could feel her against my fallopian tubes
pushing   the small yolk of   wanting

but hurled back to Canada   to Canadians
like a harsh beam of a flashlight
lighting the dark of a forest
shining it to meet the stars   seeing for the first time
how much there is I cannot reach
except with my mind

and left myself in Canada and you in Turkey
something unfinished like a dove in mid-flight
taken in the talons of passion   stilled
falling into nowhere and everywhere in one moment

Escaping

One day out of every four
I call you, in Istanbul, pretend
you live down the block;
I say nothing as you repeat,
Efendem, several times before you hang up.

One day out of every four
the Virgin comes to me.
The dust from Efes covering her hair;
she lights candles in my bedroom,
spreads roses over my closed eyes.
The sweet, strong scent of flowers
in the thick smoke filled room,
in a house that is not my own.

One day out of every four
I make it rain.

One day out of every four
I tell you, *I love you.*
The words travel on the thin air of desire
from Canada to Turkey.
The words: *I love you* become tourists and strangers;
they find you at Tevkifhâne in Sultanahmet.
Like soap bubbles they plaster themselves
against your skin, the ticklish spot
behind your thighs and sigh as you stir
against them, in the early morning,
elma çay still damp on your lips.

One day out of every four
I curse my family,
from my mother to the ancestor
who carried relics
from the Franklin Expedition
in a leather pouch.

One day out of every four
I try to fly.

One day out of every four
I pretend you have no hold on me,
pretend I can walk away from you,
I won't feel you like a drowning,
the last bit of air – escaping.

The Sound of a Violin

rebecca married the stag, the one
who looked like her in the mirror
and ran without touching the ground
cloven hoof against pale fingers
white musk of his mouth tickling
the blue veined rivers of her arms

and he left her timid and cowering
trying to make her feet touch the ground
limping over water and through rain
with the rubber-willed sole of her spirit
and a poet in the mountains of Alberta
said she reminded him of a deer
as if she kept one alabastered hand poised
above the door handle and her eyes
cratered and old like a stone

she wanted to show the poet
the shape of her feet how God
must have begun building her
and after he'd shaped two cloven hoofs
forgot what he was making
and built a woman with pale, blue skin

instead she limped down carpeted hallways
laid herself down to sleep dreaming herself
remade and running each long tendon
stretched and strung out to make a whisper
like the sound of a violin

After the Rain
> *after Lorna Crozier's poem "Noah's Wife"*

At first I thought I loved
the dragonflies best,
for they swept around my head
and hung in my hair
like elaborate decoration.
I wanted to bend their thin
reed bodies into my braids,
silencing their wings even though
I heard nothing above the rain.

Instead it was the black birds I loved best.
They came to the ark last;
the female perched on the mast above my head.
Her eyes the smooth, mirrored
surface of the first stone of rain.
And he for the first few hours,
after the water covered all he knew,
flew above the ark,
and when he landed beside her
it was with curiosity,
and not resignation.

The constant chatter of rain
soothed me, lulled me to sleep.
Even at the first light of day
the rain stroked my hair,
washed my face.

During those long days
my husband said little,
and cowered in the back of the boat
making the horses nervous.
After the rain, the crows flew
level at my shoulder as the ark
drifted along in the black
water of loneliness.
They said to me, *Call, call.*
The first sound I heard in the quiet
of the first day without rain.

And as my husband sent
dove after dove from the ark,
into the bright sunlight
of another day, it was the crows
who brought me comfort
in the dark folds of their wings.

The ark, now, is barely even memory,
but I still know the crows as if they live
inside me, as my children did,
their wings fluttering against my womb
like the constant beating of rain.
Every night since we've left the ark
they fly to me under the red belly of the sun,
when I call them by name.
And like me, regardless of the dry
heat of another day,
drops from the long rain
cover their wings and cover
my long, dark hair.

In the Absence of God

He descended graceful
as the blink of God's eye,
and my wings at my back spread,
as if I, too, would begin
the long descent into emptiness.

I wanted to follow him.

And when God began the odd,
seemingly unbounded making of earth,
with the boring task of each blade of grass,
each kernel of wheat,
I slipped out unnoticed, and fell.
Feeling, what he may have felt,
the rapid and infinite fall from grace.
And his name on my lips like the red
God gave to the apples in the east end
of the Garden of Eden.
The colour God called wisdom.

And as my feet felt the solid of what had been made,
there was light, and Lucifer said my name and asked:
Have you followed me?
I knew it was his pride which couldn't forgive me,
and when God reached out and pulled me home,
I was ashamed to realize I'd betrayed
the two I loved best.

On the Seventh day God rested,
we wondered at what he'd made
in our image. He called the man Adam
and the woman, he named her Lilith.
I could see inside Lilith, knew she was made
from a dark clay; the darkness I understood
but couldn't comprehend.
I favoured her for it, for like Lucifer
she accepted her sin without shame,
wore it like the colours found
in the folds of an owl's wings.

When Lilith was banned from Eden
I went to her, and said to the Maker of heaven and earth,
I, too, am a woman and she is made in my image.
I was the one to stand, unnoticed by her side,
and bear witness to the first woman's grief.
It was after Lilith's expulsion that Lucifer
called God, and in my innocence,
I believed Lucifer had *followed me,*
but he'd come to claim the speck of dust
God created; I waited for him to speak my name,
and when he did it was the movement
of leaves over the serpent's head and he said,
Gabriel, would you mind if I married Lilith?

I grieved with the silence of an owl in flight.
The one creation which amazed me above all others.
Touched me more than Lilith, Adam,
or even the woman made from his rib,
filled me with the wonder I saw on Cain's face
when his mother carried his mark
on her heart, and on her tongue for his pain.
I, like Lot's wife, always turned to look,
felt the wings more than they could be heard.
Just as Lot's wife felt the tremor in the air,
and turned to see the last of Sodom.
I was one of the twelve thousand angels of destruction
who descended with God to cover the city in sulphur;
to turn the Sodomites to pillars.
Our wings on the air above Sodom, silent
as owls in flight; silent as my grief which moved
endlessly over the millennia of time for the marriage
of Lilith and Lucifer wedded as they were,
in the orange fire, in the absence of God.

The Wing of God named Noah

The first time I was born
in the days when God filled up everything,
with fear as tangible as hard seeds
of a pomegranate,
he called rain. And it came down
in sheets as solid and pliable as flesh.
The drops stung like a lover's fist,
the fist of God, the Rabbi said,
and clicked his tongue at us.
Though he'd been the one who laughed
hardest at Noah and the planks of wood.
None of us laughed now. Our punishment
sweetened as we watched animals offered space
and comfort under the wing of God named Noah.

What was it like for them, in the ark
to hear us? I, too, pounded at the door
of the great boat until my knuckles bled,
thinking in my madness: No one can drink
with such thirst. And I held my face heavenward
drank until I was full. I wouldn't give up,
couldn't accept my fate so easily, and I raised my voice
above the voice of God. I called out to Noah's oldest son,
Shem, who had loved me once. He had met me in the orchards
with myrrh at his fingertips and daisies in his hands.
He looked out from the window of the great boat
holding now the breath of life, moved his mouth
in the shape of my name, and I was pulled from the ark
as if I were no more than a small pebble
at the mercy of a strong-willed child.

I moved past all I knew, the young men
who had called my name in the evening heat,
their eyes large and unmoving, their voices stilled.
My sister's arms tightly wrapped around her third child
taken by the flame of rain, her mouth circular
with surprise, frozen as if she'd been made of stone.
I reached my hand slowly toward her shawl
felt the cotton tangled in my fingers, then gone.
I wondered as the birds flew higher and higher
how did Noah know which two to pick,
Or was it all chance? Did he see into their hearts?
Know the beat of purity and honesty,
or did he guess? Did he care? Bundled up, as he was,
in the wooden hands of God. Motionless against mercy.

I survived without spite or pride. I floated endlessly it seemed
from the orange light of morning into the white
light of night; I simply refused to be taken,
until the rain spoke to me on the twenty-third day
of the third month, when the moon rose round and full.
And I was lulled by the great waters which bathed me;
I dreamt myself back to my beginnings.
Let the rain take me with his hands, whispering,
his mouth pulling at my clothes until I was
                                        silenced.

The world has too much colour

He wants me to leave Mexico,
but I can't, I have to stay here.
He thinks I'm in love with Nando,
but I'm in love with the muted colours
of Nando's religion, with the beggars
and children on the corners
selling flowers and rosaries
for the dead; I'm in love with Mexico.

They found me in the market, and he wants
to take me back, home, to Canada.
But I am not myself, I bleed from the wounds of Christ,
and God calls me by another name in the evenings.
Last night I slept in the Virgin's arms,
she placed rose petals over my eyes.
He asks if I'd like to go to a monastery,
in Montréal, where they make cheese and honey.

I like the difference between him and Nando.
The dark and the light is delicious.
I like wearing the two of them,
but now he seems so startled white,
so breathtakingly translucent how can I enjoy him?

I have nothing. I don't know how to dress myself.
The world has too much colour.
I wear rags and arrange them in flattering patterns;
I dream of Christ descending, his arms held open, wide,
        falling into my body.

Smell Violets

I remember the sweet perfume of violets,
and a Latino child reaching his hands
towards my face to cover me in Christ's blood.
It was Nando who said he always smelt violets
when someone bled from the five wounds of Christ.
I was with his sister, Maria, when I disappeared;
we had been in a church in the country
where a wooden Virgin wept.
Nando found me in a small café drinking Coke
and watching MTV; he took me home,
and covered me with his warm brown skin,
but my flesh never came alive and I closed my thighs
only to wake up standing beside Pilate
and a flogged Christ who asked, *Will you die for me?*
Will you die for me?

God Made Fruit

I am the woman who has loved you well,
if somewhat distantly but, you must know,
certainly no less than if I'd been the one
you'd allowed to lie beside you during the long winters.
And if I had been there as you married,
it isn't myself I ever imagined dressed and standing
so stoic in white, but rather buckets filled
with salmonberries, saskatoons, blueberries,
raspberries, plums, peaches, and oranges;
for you, the one I have loved before and after all others,
baskets overflowing with kiwis, apples, apricots,
mulberries, cranberries, melons and mangos.

I couldn't stop there because my desire for you
has always intoxicated me; I have found you
sweet and tart on my tongue.
As teenagers we spent our summer afternoons
in the fields of northern Saskatchewan.
Our hands pricked raw and our tongues
glazed red with choke-cherries.
I've always liked such a round bud,
one that rolls along the tongue promising
endless miles of sweetness and succulent moisture,
as if it'll end all thirst, and yet as soon as you pop
the tender skin with your teeth the juice expands
into a quiet scream. The choke-cherry steals
all the saliva from the mouth and then tosses
itself down the throat leaving you parched
and disoriented, believing no matter where you are
your arms are flayed wide in fields
of rhubarb and alfalfa.

For you, the first of all my lovers and the man
I have dreamt of sleeping and awake, I'd give away
boysenberry with its burgundy flesh to tempt you back
again and again; cracked halves of pomegranates,
seeds of fuschia in beds of white linen;
green and yellow pears to rest in your hands,
the stringy white meat to quarter, to section,
to leave its juice sickly, sweet and sticky on your chin.

I would counsel you to wed cherries –
blood red and bursting – each bite a conundrum,
even the wedding guests would shoot cherry pits
ludicrously across the nave. Hail Marys and Our Fathers
forgotten, and rosaries left dangling on the pews.
The flower girls would come carrying grapes,
green, maroon and rust some seedless and some not.
The bridesmaids would offer thick slices of watermelon
and cups filled with apple seeds.

For you, man who has torn me asunder, I'd gather
blackberries in my hands, throw them in the air
to circle you the round, living, blood of confetti.

On Marrying a Dragon

If I married a dragon I'd invite all my relatives
even the ones who are dead.
Highlanders would come carrying Celtic crosses
and swords they could barely lift.
My dead relatives from the Lowlands,
as Highlanders seldom die, would carry baskets
filled with fruit and heather from the fields.
I'd want a simple ceremony,
and when the fruit was ripe enough
for the grapes to burst and leave juice
covering the wedding guests,
and seeds lying by my feet, some with plump,
grape-flesh still hanging,
he'd place a silver ring on my finger.
A token I'd wear all the days of my life,
and I'll live a long time: I take after the Highlander side.

Yes, I'd marry a dragon; for you see
I'm born in the year of the dragon,
and I've never been frightened of fire,
not even as a child when the neighbour's house
burst into flames which flickered out the windows
and licked at the sky.

If I married a dragon I'd never have to get
another government or secretarial job.
I could make elaborate tapestries all day
and he'd come home in the evenings
after terrorizing lands I've never seen.
I would never have to tell him I love him;
never have to doubt his faithfulness; never have to play bridge.
Instead I could listen when he called out in his raspy voice,
Lower the moat, or whatever it is he'd say.

After I've married a dragon all my freckles
will darken like the coat of a Bay;
my red hair will turn even brighter, becoming
the shades of indigo, white and the reds found only in fire.
I'll be lazy in the mornings and slink out of bed like a snake;
spend hours brushing my hair, pinning it up, taking it down.
Until I, too, grow forest green wings from my shoulder blades
and can push fire from my mouth.

Marrying Snails
   with thanks to Aislinn P. Hunter

One would never be enough.
I would have to marry several,
maybe even more.
Line them all up
tucked over the vein ridges
of leaves on a full moon.
      Possibly marrying them only
during an Indian summer;
however, being Indian, every summer
is Indian summer.
I know I'd be disappointed.
They'd all blend eventually,
and soon enough I wouldn't be able
to tell any of them apart.
Possibly I'd forget names
and have to resort to calling
them all *Babe*, or some other
equally trite form of affection.
It wouldn't be long before one
or possibly all of them (binding
together in the face of a common enemy)
would ask why I'd married them to begin with,
and I would never have an answer.
Wouldn't be able to tell them
how, when they sleep,
I touch each of them with my tongue,
curling it along their spiralled indifference;
finding no beginning and no end
to the motion; being Indian, for me,
means suffering from a great unrest.
The desire for a different place
to set my feet down every morning,
to lay my head on every night
the beginning and end irrelevant

only the constant motion of their spirals
matter to me. They intoxicate me
with the promise of movement
as sweet as molasses. Shame,
how I hate what I love the most.

On Marrying the Last Unicorn

By the time he came to me
I was an old woman,
my virginity lost as if I misplaced it
with baskets for gathering berries
in the cold, damp of the cellar.

He spoke to me, as I bent over the well hauling water,
he was the last of them, he said.
And I couldn't offer compassion to a unicorn.
I wrapped my hands round the rope;
remembered how I always said,
Go. Leave; remembered I was the first
to help lovers with their bags to the door.
I didn't care. Nothing's forever, that's what I thought,
and they were gone like the ripple of a white flag
on the maypole which waves *I surrender.*
So I planted, harvested, and noticed as I stretched,
one spring day, to gather apple blossoms
 – I was an old woman.

I laughed when he told me what he wanted.
Really laughed; I forgot the well, the water,
forgot he was the last of them.
I doubled over laughed and laughed

until my hair turned the colour of honey,
and my age spots turned to freckles.
I stood and laughed as my hands got young,
my legs got strong, and my spine got straight.
Then I offered him something to drink,
and as he hung his head to my outstretched hands
I said, *Yes.*

Apple Seeds

I'm lonely and tired of blowing
ashes from your endless cigarettes
off my endless drafts of poetry

I'm certain I've as many poems
as I do eggs, and both run out of me
at spaced intervals following
some pattern the moon has set

I don't want to lose anything
every cycle makes me tired
anaemic with grief
I can do nothing
but put another pad
on the crotch of my underwear
put more paper in the printer
hope what I'm losing isn't the best
of me

watch as my body
empties itself
of eggs and poetry

you don't care why should you
you don't want children
and even if you did
you could have them
numerous little tadpoles
swell in your body
you will never run out

on the road between
Rae and Yellowknife you give me
the seeds from your green apple
I put them in my pocket,

four apple seeds,
will a fine poem come for me
while there is still time

Up Against the Wall, Mother
for Aislinn P. Hunter

... and you say, *I'm up against the wall,
Mother,* but she doesn't answer.
She turns away and offers you
pottery well formed,
fitted like a young boy's armpits,
hollowed like chalices
and it doesn't matter how beautiful,
you always want to know its function.

*Yes, yes, yes a beautiful pitcher,
but how well does it pour?*

How much will it hold, how far can you fill it?
You take it always
too far and it spills over,
and you lean against that wall,
push your back against it;
you won't admit to over-flow.
You ignore the signs
that say, *This is too much.*
You whisper, *Not enough, not enough, too much.*

You are aligned up against the wall,
filled to the even mark, and
you pour so well.

Birthmarks

I have two: the first a round
dot in the centre of my right calf.
Carmel-coloured, my lover said,
it tastes of peanut butter cookies.
I loved it long ago
as a child when I would twirl
and dance and shake my booty.

The other birthmark
is unknown to me.
It hides between hip and back.
Something which receives comments
at the beach and no notice from lovers.
It's smooth to the touch
so I can't locate it with my fingers.
I imagine it dark as milk chocolate
though, my mother says,
it's the same shade as my numerous freckles,
but unlike my freckles,
small smatterings of colour
against my pale flesh,
this mark is large and oddly shaped.
I imagine it's untameable.
Reminds me of the coat
of an Appaloosa or the speckled wings of hawk.

My love for this second birthmark
is hidden and shy.
I move awkward steps around it
and wear dark coffee coloured coats
to make it feel at home,
but every now and then it shakes off
the presence of two-legged beasts.
Wants to run wild as fresh horses
in the fields; it flirts when I'm not looking
and gives my hips that extra (whiplash) swing.
It's a mature and sophisticated birthmark
with a wink and a nudge.
It's too old to shake its booty
but it loves to strut its stuff.

you bring out the good girl in me
  After Sandra Cisneros

the sock hops, checkered skirts,
neck-tie, catholic girl in me
the rosary in the pocket, Eucharist
on the lips and ashes on the forehead in me
you do, you do,
you bring out the good girl in me
the lolita-wearin'-sunglasses,
hair in a pony tail swingin'
side to side in me
you bring out the cherry red
lollipop lickin' in me, yes
you do, yes you do
bring out the good girl in me
you make me want to twist & shout
turn & spin even spit & run
you do, you do
I swear it's true
you bring out the good girl in me

In the Presence of Your Heart

Your heart was born in Argentina
it beats out Latin rhythms
murmurs the tango and the mariachi
is frightened of Fascists
hides the switchblade in the boot
and the pistol in the pocket

Your heart is the butterfly in my mouth
the moth against my tongue
the wings cooling my flesh
after the nights filled with tequila
and the spitfire draw of your voice

Your heart is the indigo of God
and the fire-engine red of debauchery

In the presence of your heart
my will curls like my fist
while I sleep with my dreams
lit against closed eyes

In the presence of your heart
my arms and legs leap
pulling me like the acrobats
in a Paris circus
and breath pulls itself out
like I've been caught in mid-air
flying the trapeze

Your heart's mysterious
it's barely met my own,
and I cover my emotions
as a Bedouin woman covers her hair
in the presence of men.

Your heart is the indigo of God
the fire red of debauchery
and my own is caught mid-air
still for a moment before
it begins the long descent.

I swear it to you

Trust me, I swear it to you,
love of my long hair,
man of my dreams.
        Your mouth,
        fingers,
        breath,
kissing my heart, kissing me asunder.
I swear it, trust me, I swear it to you.
Love of my piano fingers, love
of my nubile, belt buckling agility,
love of my near-sighted stare,
        squint of eyes
        and rise of brows,
trust me, I swear it, trust me.
Lover of my flesh,
slope of belly, rise of breasts,
lover of my pale skin and clean teeth,
lover of my lily-white limbs,
freckled back and birthmarks
        count them there are two,
I swear you, you, can trust me.
You, the lover of my rages
insane and manic; love of my weeping,
moaning, frantic crying, wringing of hands,
shaking of breath, and lover of my
light conversation, slight pauses,
thick silences,   kiss me,
kiss me asunder.
You know, what I do with my body,
this body, you love with your hands,
and where I place my mouth,
my fingers and breasts,
what I do with my body, this body,
this body of mine who I choose

to give myself to how many times
can I tell you I choose you.
Trust me, I swear, trust me it's true.

Cover Me with Kisses

You leave me in the truck
as you go off into the thicket of trees.
I watch you go,
with your gun and your hunger,
and I touch the leather of these seats,
turn up the stereo,

remember waiting here, waiting
here for you or someone else like you
to come back from the forest
with flesh; my brother taught you
to hunt and still you're
too good at it.

I don't eat meat except in restaurants,
where it's been shot up with hormones,
and vitamins and is so tameable I can't
taste anything wild.

You don't hurry; you don't rush;
you don't remember me in the truck,
waiting and watching deer tip-toe
across the small dirt road,
and I nod my head as they pass.

I sit in the truck,
imagine you doing battle
with the forest, hacking your way
to a castle, to bend, kiss, touch,
awaken Snow White or Sleeping Beauty.
That would be an admirable thing to do
on a Saturday with your hunting license
tucked in those stupid overalls.

You come through the forest,
only your gun in your hands,
and you sit beside me in the truck,
smiling and randy because the thought
of killing does that to you.
You cover me with kisses,
but you can't wake me up.

Part 3: Too Small to Remember

In the end, the edges of memory
are licked smooth
by the coarse tongue of time,
wiped clean.
All you did was beautiful, and good.

– Karen Connelly

What I want

I want to come home after school and find my mother at home; not at work, not waitressing at The Lodge, not giving the tourists gas at the Esso, not working afternoons at the Bank of Montreal. I want her home, wearing dresses like Lynette's mother and baking cookies like Mrs. Nymon.

I want to grow up in one town, in one house, to go to the same church every Sunday. I want to know one confession booth like my tongue knows the grooves between each of my teeth.

I want to be a cheerleader in high school and go out with Tom Houston the football star. I want to be prom queen, to get the red ribbon in the May Ball Rodeo for barrel racing. I want to marry my teenage sweetheart and go work on the ranch with him. I'll bake apple pies.

I want one best friend to tell my secrets, wishes and hopes to; to grow up with, to stand beside when she gets married. I want to visit her in the hospital, bringing bright yellow roses each time she gives birth. I'll play Bingo with her on Saturday nights when our husbands are off volunteering for the local Fire Department. I want us to grow old together, sit barefoot in the hot sun drinking lemonade.

I want to give birth to three children and raise them in this village my mother took me away from. I want them to play on Mississippi log, hike up to Porcupine's cave, to know the feel of stirrup, bit and bridle. I want them to know their family, to know their place in the world and to belong.

My mother taught me

My mother taught me how to tell the truth, not to the teenage girls who worked at the Pinetree and caught me nipping penny candy, but to myself. Made me tell the truth to myself the way she made the colour of my eyes. Made me like I was a soft form of clay she shaped with her will and never had to touch.

My mother taught me how to move; not how to dance or swing my hips, not how to pirouette or arabesque, but how to pack, tape boxes, disconnect the hydro and telephone. She taught me how to let go.

She taught me how to swim; not the clear, clean strokes of those not afraid of the water, but the fierce kick of those barely moving at all. She taught me to choke in air and water at the same time to gurgle, fight, grin and bear it all.

My mother taught me how to laugh; not to whisper laughter out. Not a small, dainty, tinkling laugh but a laugh which shakes the room. To toss back my head, let it roll up from deep within me, let it gain momentum as it comes, let it shake and tip and topple my vocal chords. I let laughter become everything, let it roll and roar and dance and bring me the sweetest of pleasure till my face turns pink and I can see stars in front of my eyes.

She taught me how to hug; not the cool embrace with a light pat on the back. No, my mother taught me to pull those I love in close, wrap my arms around them. Kiss their cheeks, give them an extra squeeze. Let go.

She taught me how to drive in all kinds of weather, in strange cities (without a map), fast in reverse and in city limits, slow and leisurely in the country. My mother taught me to pack a lunch, travel with fruit, with Hank Williams, Patsy Cline and Neil Diamond at full blast, to sing along with all the tunes.

My mother taught me how to believe in God. To run my tongue over his eyelashes, to braid his hair. To lie down in his bed when I'm tired, so he can cover me in angel wings and bathe my feet, kiss my hands. She taught me the rosary, the skip of beads against fingers, the cluck of tongue on prayer. She taught me how to drink his blood, eat his flesh, rejoice at his dying, sing his praise. She taught me hope, faith and love. Love with an open embrace; my mother taught me to let go.

I want to go home

I want to go home, to crawl into the body I owned as a child.

When I get there I'll climb trees with Kaug and Ed. I'll wrestle Tim down on the autumn grass of the elementary school. I'll ride my bicycle around the block – past the Pinetree, through the park, swing past my Auntie Joyce's house, past the elementary school, up to my grandma's house.

When I get there I'll help take the clothes off the line, copy her and stick the pegs in my mouth and keep on talking. We'll gather beets, potatoes, carrots, and green peas from her garden. She'll tell me what ugly fingernails I have, and ask why I act like a lumberjack.

My mother'll come home from one of her three jobs, and she and grandma will drink coffee in the kitchen. Me and my brother will go outside and stack the wood while my grandfather chops it. My grandpa will tell me what a tough little girl I am, just like a lumberjack.

And in the evening before I go to bed I'll say my prayers with my mother, and sink down into the flannel and guilt of the women who raise me.

I loved her

I grew up in the Cariboo. I learned to ride horses, change tires, fight like a boy, climb trees, pick crab apples (so good, so sour). I learned to do the wash in the old wringer washers, and I never got my hand caught. I learned to work hard, to never buckle under the load, to keep on going, to walk proud, to be respectful of my elders, believe in God, honour my mother, spit on my father (lousy son of a bitch). I learned to hunt like the boys. Where I grew up they taught me not to be squeamish. It never mattered if I couldn't quite keep up, I could hold my own.

I never turned away from dead animals my grandpa brought home. I helped him lift them from the back of the truck and helped him haul them into the shed. I watched as he skinned them, nailed them to plywood, sometimes I helped. I was only bothered once, my cousins, Edward, Kaug, and Tim, hauled me outside to come look at the cougar Grandpa shot. Then they pointed at the cougar's mouth where she'd bit down on her tongue when she was hit. Bit down. Bit all the way through. Her thin, sharp, white tooth glistening at the other end. I loved her.

When my brother was eleven he shot a whisky-jack with his pellet gun. He came into the house to get me. I told him he'd have to finish her off, we couldn't leave her almost dead. He said, he couldn't. So I bit down and killed that tiny bird.

I bit down, could feel her thin, sharp tooth at the other end.

Compass
for Katy Ellis

Katy has a compass tattooed just above her left breast. I keep a compass in my blood, if I need to know where I am I look at my feet.

Katy has maps not only on paper, but in her mind. When she and Richard came back from Mexico she described the trip so well I could see it laid out before me. The long roads shining red on the white backdrop, each town glistening like the black pupil of Katy's eyes. She tattooed her compass over her heart because she needs to know how to get there.

When I'm dead

When I'm dead my mother will hold me, caress me, cleanse me. She'll take a warm, damp cloth and wash my face, my chest bone, my breasts, the freckles over my arms and hands; she'll bend and kiss my fingers. She'll wash my back, praising spine and shoulder bones. She'll soap the width of my hips and the birthmarks – one between hip and back and the other at the centre of my calf.

My mother will make a bed for me, put the weight of time on my bones the way living has not; my mother will crystallize me between amber the way she built me in her womb. My mother will bury me between rock and sand.

She'll bring me milk and cookies and sing to me every Sunday afternoon on her way home from church. She'll pour holy water she's stolen from the altar over my grave to water the lilies. She'll read from the Old Testament in her strong, gentle voice and I'll say the words with her. Whisper them from between limestone and quartz.

When I'm dead my mother and I will have all the time in the world to love one another. I'll always be her baby girl, and she'll bring me macadamia nuts on Tuesdays and tell me what she saw at the movies. We won't argue or disagree. She'll tell me I'm full of beans while she eats peanuts on Wednesdays and I'll chuckle from deep beneath the soil.

My mother will love me as she couldn't when I was alive. She'll praise every scar, each rise of breast, roundness of hip; she won't turn away. She'll kiss each mound of eye, hold me like she held me in her womb when I was too small for her to remember.

Acknowledgments

Poems in this collection have previously appeared or will appear in: *Prism International, Fiddlehead, Grain, Northernher, The Inner Harbour Review, Tessera, Wascana Review, NeWest Review, Room of One's Own* and in the anthologies: *The Colour of Resistance*, *Breathing Fire*, and *A Shade of Spring*.

The title of "having loved that country like blood burst in the brain" is from a poem by Aislinn P. Hunter.

The title of "I Have Lived Here Since the World Began" is from the book by Arthur J. Ray with the same title.

The last two lines of "Apple Seeds" is a variation from two lines in a poem by Confucius known as "Ripe Plums are Falling".

This book could not have been written without the financial support of the Canada Council and the Northwest Territories Art Council. I would like to thank my editor, Patrick Lane, for his gracious support. Thanks also to Derk Wynand, Lorna Crozier, Margaret Hollingsworth, Brian Hendricks, Aislinn P. Hunter, Line Gagnon, Katy Ellis, Walter Brown, Easton (India) Saravanja, Deborah Rossouw, Billeh Nickerson, and Rebecca Fredrickson.

Mahsi cho to Richard Van Camp and special thanks to my mother, Mazie Nelson, and my brother, Kevin MacLeod, for their love and support.